On Mother and Fatherland

Bożena Keff

Translated from the Polish
by Benjamin Paloff and Alissa Valles

MadHat Press
Asheville, North Carolina

MadHat Press
MadHat Incorporated
PO Box 8364, Asheville, NC 28814

The Library of Congress has assigned
this edition a Control Number of
2017910062

ISBN 978-1-941196-52-6 (paperback)

Portions of this book have previously appeared in *PEN America: A
Journal for Writers and Readers, Scattering the Dark: An Anthology of
Polish Women Poets,* and *Little Star.* Grateful acknowledgement is
made to Bill Martin, Karen Kovacik and Ann Kjellberg and to the
Polish Book Institute (under the direction of Grzegorz Gauden),
which gave initial support to this project through the Sample
Translations program.

Cover art by Marc Vincenz
Cover design by Marc Vincenz
Book design by MadHat Press

www.MadHat-Press.com

First Printing

TABLE OF CONTENTS

Epilogue

*

I have this dream I'm holding—standing in a train station—
holding a smallish something, like a child, a few years old,
only not a child, a shaggy, wailing mass,
it twists it squirms, the blood on tufts,
I have to hold on, shield it from harm, and why   *who*
        knows,
it's like I was shocked into it; I feel a little sick,
a little sorry. It's like there's a wound here, and beside it the
        bloodstained tufts,
it reeks of burning, it stiffens, it squirms, I can barely hold on,
it's constantly wailing, where does it get the air,
it deafens it blinds. Focused and frantic, I'm trying not to let go,
what's happening I don't know, this thing
I thought I'd have for a minute,
but now I see no one's coming to take it off my hands,
the trains are leaving, people passing,
and I'm standing here waiting for what   who knows.

PART I
THE LAMENT
SINCE TIME IMMEMORIAL

The Aftertaste of Empty

Chorus
The mother's lament since time immemorial, her eternal
oi moi oi moi
the ancient history of her suffering, of which there can be
    no doubt.

Narratrix
Her life story, in the bygone era of Mother and Family,
before the war,
her tale of tales from the war,
the tale of her escape rescue death and the Jewish descent
    into the subhuman;

she's made nothing up, there are facts archives films
        documents,
she says *something's wrong with me,* a belly ache,
I have this aftertaste of corpse and then emptiness—
burp

Chorus
Oi moi oi moi
from vacuum into void
she gave birth to a child.

Narratrix
To have a family, not to be alone,

her child is forever Her Mother's Child,
her mother is *The Mother,* after all. As The Mother,
a woman's not lost in the world
and gets a kind of identity.

Chorus
The daughter just has no words for
how empty how boring how old her mother is,
oi moi tyraness of emptiness!
Never listens, sees whatever, feels what she feels like
        feeling,
words fail with her, words fail for her, nothing gets
        through,
and that daughter, nothing's ever good enough for her!

Narratrix
So the daughter is a *Poet.*
There's nothing she can't express!

Part II
The Visit and Other Recollections

Way Down in the Mississippi Delta

Aura (The Daughter): A Monologue

Way down in the Mississippi Delta, darkness, stifling
       fumes; the current
carries me half-conscious on a rotting raft and is sure
to carry me to her apartment on Mordechai
Anielewicz. I can't pull out of it,
can't swing on vines out of here and into the sky, to a plane
that just happens to be flying to the world outside; here
       it's Either/Or,
Either (you're here)/Or (you're here). The gate now opens
       before me,
and look: that's me stepping into the same river as the day
       before yesterday—

*

only I'm too spent to scramble up the bank, change my
       dress,
slap on my sandals and walk away,
leave her to herself—leave me to myself—
maybe, I think, die—maybe let it go. I don't ask *what*
       anymore,
this is no place for reflection. Consider, Gentle Passer-by,
that I was already caught in the current
when still in the belly of Fate. Who now parts the
       creaking
iron gate, beyond which
there should be something,

7

an alleged interior;
who opens the door, and I, as foretold, enter
with a hope I don't really think I have.

Meter's Song: By My Lonesome
(the mother sings bass)

By my lonesome in my four walls in these four walls alone
but what do you care that your mother's alone in her four walls
what's my life to you what would you know about my life will you
make it your business to understand my tragic
life my awful life or even just my infection from hell
what's it to you. You're barely here before you want to go.
I'm sure
you have more interesting things going on than your mother
          or her life.

Oh, I'm sure, I don't doubt it, of course you do—

Bożena Keff

Meter's Song: Got Out of Lvov
(the mother sings alto)

I got out of Lvov in a summer dress and with nothing but
          that dress
and a small suitcase with underwear blouses two skirts
that later saved my life when I traded them for kasha,
I was in sandals, that's how I got on the truck
and left
my mother, my sister her husband their child my uncle my aunt
I had no idea it didn't occur to me
when I came back there'd be nobody left,
just ruins—

Aura
And so today we find ourselves at this portion of the Oral
          Testament,
where she abandoned her mother to save herself.
Mark, Gentle Passer-by, this moment
of grave import—

Lara Croft

Narratrix
In the backwaters of depression she lies half-sunken, her
    open maw
full of complaint—sometimes a tongue of hot lava—
    sometimes a scattering
of cold ash from the archives of the Jewish Historical
    Institute,
where, sorting through the shot and the gassed,
she stumbled on something.
"I found," says she, looking
straight into the void (which is me, on a chair), "a document.
My mother was killed in a forest outside Lvov.
She was shot in the forest. Half a century, and I didn't know."

*

For half a century she didn't know, and now she knows.
And she speaks of it in the presence of a random witness.
In point of fact, a brunette in crocodile-skin gloves,
agent from the world of make-believe, Lara Croft, or some
    such,
who's firing up her Cessna in Hawaii when an old maid
in a threadbare cloak gets snagged in the propeller. Lara
    climbs out
to help the poor thing, who, eyes cast into the void,
    informs her
that half a century ago her mother was shot in the forest.

"How horrible!"
cried Lara, for she is not without a heart.

Meter's Song: I Ain't Been Right Since Morning Light
(the mother sings soprano)

I ain't been right since morning light and it hurts here and here
I ain't been right
don't know what's wrong, didn't eat this whole month long,
     can't keep nothing
down
have to gnaw at this dry roll barely sipping at my gruel
didn't eat nothing but a scrap of boiled chicken maybe like
     last year
every day I'm blocked up, run down and done,
if this grub's not right there's something wrong with me
goddamn infection in these four walls
forever and ever, amen—

Bożena Keff

Little Aura's Song: By the Rivers of Babylon (1)

Aura

*By the rivers of the Babylonian wasteland there I sat down
not weeping not striking up the band not remembering
because what would there be for me to remember maybe
that by the rivers of the wasteland there I sat down
not weeping not striking up the band not remembering
because what would there be for me.*

Little Aura's Song: Ecosystem

Sitting at her place I gnaw at something not listening
    while she broadcasts
since time immemorial that broadcast has annihilated me,
I don't exist here as I, I'm a sound booth
or a pond in the woods where voices ring clear,
no more left of me than a fish out of water
snapping its mute jaws, no!, no!, and again, snap, no!
But what good is that. My attitude stems from impotence
and won't get me anywhere,
no past for me here, no future.
Spiritually, things are looking pretty bad. Corporeally,
    much worse.
Already I'm half-dead and empty, but mother hasn't had
    enough,
the suckling still wants to suck its story, howl it out—

Master Frodo, be careful,
don't let the dead things pull you into the marshes!
Say what you want, Master Frodo's going down,
Master Frodo's future's got death written all over it.

Little Aura's Song: Way Down in My Mother's Mississippi

I'm sitting at my mother's in the swamp,
crunch crunch crunching crackers and sipping water,
hey, I'm just a little mammal. My name is Khora.
You can bet
I'm a little shit. My being here is like a band-aid or a pill,
who can say no to a victim, who can say no to The Mother,
not that she wants to know who I am. Korusha.
Aura, her little daughtusha.
I'm flipping through *Time* amidst static
tuned to frequency of Upper Respiratory Infection
or History or Labor *(big boss man, bastard, thinks he can
        walk all over me),*
sitting at the radio jammer, reading about film festivals
in Berlin or Cannes. To really make a break for it!
Really change reality,
all that effort, money, someone else's part in your make-
        believe,
like it's for real. This year, Polanski
and his *Pianist*. When the lights go up, the applause
        washes away the shame and disgrace,
and when all's said and done you're more artist than Jew,
it's always been this way, I totally get it.

Part III
The Tale of Aura and Her Meter

Time Came, Her Daughter

Narratrix
Time came, her daughter wanted to go out into the wide
world,
gather the rosebuds of feeling and adventure. As a girl
she threw rocks through strangers' windows—it's hard to
break
your own gods' glass. They say: leave the goddess's
window alone. But
this twenty-something
planned her plans, dreamed her dreams, harbored a very
conscious hope
of getting away from her Meter. She wanted to be a
reporter, see the world,
no family, no shit to do.

And coming down from those fantasies, maybe a date,
maybe a movie, refuge of the perplexed, opening the door,
Meter was right there, a shadow on the wall, lurking in
the kitchen or bathroom,
like shackles of the past, like guard towers—

YOU! she shrieks, it's all because of YOU
that I married that loser,
I wanted YOU to have a father. Now he's gone, got
himself some girl.
So now you'll be my husband, my mother-and-father,

because it was all because of you, for you, all for you!
And you don't even have the sense of family
to know what's owed your mother.
She crashes around the kitchen drawer for a knife to stab
     and kill
herself, all for this child, this evil, this guilty party.
To lay this on her, too, standing over her mother's body,
reduced to ashes!

*

The child is stricken, desolate, guts stomach heart
pressed into a block of ice,
on her face a crooked, ironic smile at *that idiot,*
which will remain with her forever, a mark of higher
     intelligence
and all-purpose *kiss my ass.*

Meter's Song: You Double-Crossing Bitch
(the mother sings soprano)

You double-crossing bitch! My one salvation!
Why have you forsaken me in Death
Valley? Instead of abiding here with me
And listening to my guts wrench, my inner life spills over
From one disaster to another, to which you have been
      called as witness,
Khora Crapora!
And this is as close as you'll get to a calling,
          gut-fucker.

The SS *Nostromo*

Narratrix
A decade later these rebellions had assumed the deep cover
of family life, which took over as a refuge from family life.
Ripley's grown up, a lot has changed, but not so much,
besides that life
aboard the family ship is great. Alien joins the crew
almost every day, several times a day. Ripley's husband, on
       his own spaceship,
is okay with that,
one mother's as good as another, sponsors her daughter's
       clothes and creams
because she'll never get it together,
Alien's always there for her, that's what The Mother's for,
taking care of her kid, though her kid has a kid of her own.

Chorus
They sometimes watch TV together.
Tata-ta-ta!—What's up with the world?
They blather on, who's killing who, yada yada yada.

Narratrix
Alien likes to see her grandson, so Ripley grants visitation
       rights,
maybe more than she'd like, just to keep Alien from going
       on about her four walls,

because it drives Ripley up them. Because she's told she's
        supposed to be a fifth,
live wall to deliver Meter from all those dead. Alien Meter
comes on Wednesday, stays till Friday, drops in on
        Saturday,
hangs around till Thursday. "Isn't my castle my mother's,
        too?"
she asks herself, Khora, Hades' wife-ora,
wooden princess. But the cosmonaut Ripley takes an
        Oresteian tack.
She asks, her back to the wall, terrified,
if Alien knows how long she plans to stay aboard,
and couldn't they settle it
like human beings.

To which Alien says, "Ri-pley! You sure know how to kick
        your mother when she's down!
For a child is bitter as bile and death!
She gives her mother an infection from hell and casts her
        to her four walls.
You're just like Hitler:
He made my life a desert of solitude, too."

Chorus of Furies
She's killed her mother! She's killed her own mother, that
        heartless little Orestes!

Narratrix

She stands in the corridor of the rocketship,
in her underwear, her underwear and a filthy shirt. The
    fuses blown,
the defrosting freezer leaks. Two days she's struggled.
She can't take any more. She gets on the bus, off to cut the
    body
down from the rafters, presumably.
She finds the body eating chicken with apple. That's one
    tough cookie.
But Ripley is no creampuff, either,
seeing as she's finally managed to knock Alien into outer
    space.

Aura

It's not like a wanted to throw her out,
I just wanted to have a little down time, like a human
    being. To hang out
with Lena or Baśka on Friday or Saturday, play with the kid,
nothing like sex is even on the menu,
just read a bit, focus on my own thing.

Chorus

But she has so many things! She's all pie in the sky!
The phantom carousel turns in her head,

and it flickers with the lights of art, adventure, fame,
      romance, genius, i.e., life.
Life magazine. Brilliant, young, easy on the eyes,
"I saw the greatest mind of my generation," her.

Narratrix
But the revolution is over. Ripley, back in the hallway,
      listening
for Alien lying in wait.
Or retreating into her capsule to sleep through the next few
years of space travel. She wracks her brains over that
      amorphous life form,
that sucking vampire,
and so she is suspended in contemplation,
this overripe infant.

Part IV
Nosferatu, Head of the Local Branch of Solidarność

Trade Unions Against Slavery

Chorus
(with a "Solidarity" flag, beginning in a round)

On a nearby school, in white paint: K.O.R. = KIKES.
Then there was a fuss, but no one painted over it. Nor did
    Aura
deny herself some hope,
she joined Trade Unions Against Slavery;
she's as engaged as can be. But how much is that,
when the Mother Church is so involved, no great freedom
    will come of it.
She sees the trenches of homegrown slavery more than
    freedom's barricades,
and besides, a lot of people blame those damn Commie
    Jews.

Narratrix
Her father, for one. Who left this life long ago
(and me, Aura sometimes thinks, but she doesn't dare
    hold it against a suicide).
She spends whole days listening to music, her heart aches,
she'd like to get a divorce and get away—far away—such a
    sick country!

They don't get their own history, they've got no identity,
no compassion, no empathy, these sometime slaves of the
        nobility,
all of whom think they're nobles. A tribe glued together
        by myth,
where individuality is *verboten.*
Every man here has to be an everyman, a son who rules
        over his wife-mother,
the Other has to be a Jew scheming in cellars.

All you ever hear is kike this, kike that, if it weren't for
        those kikes,
that Rakowski, that Urban, things would be different,
if it weren't for those kikes,
that K.O.R., those Michniks, Blumsztajns, Kurońs,
        Poland would be Polish,
wreathed in Polish truth, beauty, and goodness.
Hitler killed a lot of them, but he didn't kill them off.

Chorus

The Jews were supposedly murdered, and yet they spring
        eternal, they are so powerful they multiply in death,
quite a few neighborhoods have risen on their remains,
        churches and apartment blocks on their bones,
freeways and parks, the city of Warsaw, on Jewish ashes.
And who invited them to rot here, anyway?

It's because of them there's no sun at night,
that bad things happen to people,
that God nailed himself up
and still hangs down—

Narratrix

She's so sick of this deranged anti-Semitic country, those
        in-laws
from a small town, Jewish before the war, everybody's got
        something left from those Jews,
who "robbed them of everything!" Her in-laws sometimes
        speak
of the evacuation and the lack of meat and the sugar
        ration, it's just like today!
They talk about the culture brought to the monastery
        grounds,
when the Nazis
ordered them paved with matseva stones that have lain
        there since the war,
forty-four years,
and do not trouble the priests of the religion of love.

Nosferataura

Narratrix

O Chronos, she's in a bad way, like she's flayed,
she falls into a cosmic void, a captive,
she wants to shout: Let me out! They ask who this *me* is,
    and she doesn't know.
She panics or freezes, she wants out of that cold nothing,
but everywhere's as strange as her own mother. Everything
    affects her.
She once broke down sobbing in the street, couldn't even
    get to a doorway to hide in,
people were thinking *Poor woman They must have arrested*
    her husband
(if only they would, but that's not what she was thinking).
    Poor woman doesn't know
what to do about her crappy life, and she's over thirty,
afraid of day, afraid of night, afraid of coming, afraid of
    going.

She went to a shrink
who put her on tranquillizers and said: Time for therapy.

"Are you on good terms with your mother?"
the therapist asks, in a blue blouse, brown sweater, and
    little gold cross,
a blonde around forty, dour and impenetrable,
that's not what she needs right now.

"I dunno," Aura says, "no big drama there,
though I can't really say I'm crazy about her,
I haven't been able to go out for months, can't stand being
 at home either."

On a summer night at the cinema, formerly a synagogue,
an artist by the name of Werner Herzog and his best fiend
 Klaus Kinsky,
Nosferatu in person, brought her to an insight. Standing
 in a window, he sees his life in the light
of supreme darkness amidst cosmic Carpathian cliffs.
Leeching onto others because he has to,
it's how he plugs himself into life's bloodstream,
having dropped off centuries ago.
And that's me to a T,
Aura thinks, petrified.

Chorus

How to put it, we are both here and there; we might come
 out of our coffins and pass through walls,
but our place is in an abandoned castle,
in a castle of empty connections like veins
cut and bled long ago, and we don't even know whose
 they are—

Aura
I'm like a body by the side of the road to nowhere,
        sometimes a leg of her journey,
though the gate to that story says *No Dogs or Jews Allowed.*

I Have This Dream I'm Holding

Aura
I have this dream I'm holding—standing in a train station—
holding a smallish something, like a child, a few years old,
only not a child, a shaggy, wailing mass,
it twists, it squirms, the blood on tufts,
I have to hold on, shield it from harm, and why   who
        knows,
it's like I was shocked into it; I feel a little sick,
a little sorry. It's like there's a wound here, and beside it
        the bloodstained tufts,
it reeks of burning, it stiffens it squirms, I can barely hold on,
it's constantly wailing, where does it get the air,
it deafens it blinds. Focused and frantic I'm trying not to
        let go,
what's happening I don't know, this thing
I thought I'd have for a minute,
but now I see no one's coming to take it off my hands,
the trains are leaving, people passing,

and I'm standing here waiting for what   who knows.

Oh, My Darling Daughter

Narratrix
Oh, my darling daughter, her Meter will say
(Aura gags right away, is about to hurl),
she loves to admire her product,
her own flesh, only outside her;
what hair what skin what guts jacket heels,
she wants to know if her stomach's working well,
if her heart's pumping, how's her liver,
fifty kilos of grade A meat and more of ersatz,
with High Aural Fidelity.

PART V
THE MYTH OF GENESIS

Mother's Roots Go Back to Ancient Myth

Narratrix
Mother's roots go back to ancient myth, she herself was
    born from myth, there were no children
where such momentous things were happening. Now
    reigns the era
of peace and happy childhood. Mother tears at her story's
    skin,
at its guts, she sinks her hand into its dead belly,
you never know what she'll pull out,
typhus, deportation, starving in Volgograd, the Lvov ghetto,
Important Brother, Unimportant Sister, Stingy Aunt or
    Perfect Mother.
She swings her sweet chariot low to the hunger explosions
    death,
she howls like a hound dog, ow ow: what do you know,
    what's in that head of yours, who do you think
    you are?!

Who, me? Fuck off, hound dog!
I'm on a different page, a different channel, a different track.

Bożena Keff

Nola

Narratrix
The birthplace of the goddess is Lvov. Nola, forced out
from this nest by an angry Angra Mainyu
by the name of Hitler, had to go east, deep into Russia,
to towns and cities, all the way to the Urals, with her friend,
and it's thanks to her, she herself admits, that she survived.

Russia stretches far to the east and is being evacuated there,
except for those sent to Siberia, like Nola's brother,
        unbeknownst to her.
For now she tears forward—behind her the army of Angra
        Mainyu makes chase, infantry,
air power, armor—demons from the west in trucks, in
        jeeps,
on motorcycles, and on foot, in good boots, yet
leaving a trail of corpses, of her kind and others', and
        onward, and onward;
Nola crams herself into freight cars with everyone else,
she works in factories, sews, gets typhus, starves, and again
        flees
by train across the steppes, and over the trains the
        feathered snake of the Luftwaffe
uncurls its tail strafes locomotives stops scatters their cars,
then hunts the people, dives drives takes aim; it's Soweto
        here it's a safari!

However many the Angras Mainyu have hunted and
    devoured, they want more, they spit bones hair
    shoes,
they erect gallows light fires happily sing cry themselves
    laughing,
so radiant are they in the best of radical bestiality, the
    cadaverous decay,
they sing until their maws are filled with snow metal and
    hunger.

Chorus

As for Nola, after the war she returned to a country she
    hadn't lived in before.
To strange cities, where she would meet Aura's father, also
    from Lvov.
He'd just returned from Berlin, from the lair of Angra
    Mainyu, whom he'd crushed,
and brought back his only sewing machine for Nola.

Narratrix

With the People's Army,
"which blossoms from the hours of our friendship,"
he traversed half of Europe
and felt that he, too, belonged to the People, to the People
    of Earth, to the People of the Planet,

to Equality, Liberty, free education and agricultural
    reform,
but in time he was mortally disappointed

(though that's a different story).

*"They'll come from the west, they'll arrive in tanks and cars,
and I, and crowds, and crowds of people, onto the train,
flee to the east!"* Meter's voice screams, she's whirling within it
like a dervish, always like a top in circles.
She will never cross this time horizon.
*"But I thought my mother was safe! That my brother and
    sister!
And the whole time there was no one left."*
She says. *"No one."* She repeats, repeats
and looks into that lack of meaning—
because it's not into fate (and on this we agree).

"So you mean my grandmother," Aura says, "you mean
    my aunt."
"Grandmother?" Meter repeats. "Have you lost your
    marbles? What did these heroes
have to do with you, kid? This story happened to me.
I had to live through it.
You have Nothing to do with Anything."

Birth

(Meter's voice)
When time came to give birth, oh, such pain, I thought it
     would tear me in two.
I was out of it, I cried: *The Ghetto's on fire!*
Then the nurse
Said: I'm not going near that kike lady.
Come on, the hope was we wouldn't be seeing them
     anymore.
And here, come on—

(Aura's voice)
And so began the second half of the twentieth century
In Poland.

Part VI
Slave Plantation

The Gods Want Blood

—Viva, viva la libertad!
—Ta-ta-ta-ta!
[we hear the Commandant's footsteps]
—Mozart, *Don Giovanni*

Aura
Am I like the Aztecs or some such cannibals in believing
that without a blood sacrifice the world will end? The
         gods want blood,
or else they'll destroy the world. And me with it.
That's exactly what I believe, but about what, I don't
         know.
I don't even remember, because it's like this every day,
I don't even know as I am getting on the altar, slicing
         myself open,
tearing my heart out, fresh meat, black pudding—

choke on it, you blind, exotic idiot,
you rapist cunt!

I am an enslaved people, dark, crying into my pillow,
no history of my own, no chronicles, no permanent address.
I have nothing that is mine alone, for I haven't stopped
         deceiving myself,
I'm like delusion, like mist, like bullshit:
so maybe my mom will notice me for once?
Ask how I'm doing? And I'll say:

not great. Then she'll figure it out.
And she'll scream, once she sees the light she'll scream,
because finally she'll be The Mother, she'll scream,
because maybe she doesn't wish me slavery, pain, death:
I release you!
And she'll let go of the leash.
And I'll be free to go.

Way Down in the Mississippi Delta
(Paul Robeson sings bass)

Way down in the Mississippi Delta, where my blood's in
        the soil,
everywhere lie the bones of runaway slaves, or rather slaves
        on the run,
since it takes a while, it's rarely done. Take that writer,
        Jelinek,
always running, never run. Chained to her mother
before her death, and when her mother was gone she
        couldn't move
to pick up her own Nobel! It terrifies me to think,
is it possible that she wrote everything but that one story,
which has to be written on different material?
Such anger, such precision—and where's the freedom,
        Elfriede? where?
But better she doesn't tell me,
                        better she not answer.

And Now the Child

Narratrix

And now the child ties a rope around her neck
like a bow and waits, maybe they'll kick her out and beat
      her, let her starve—
then she's won, at least she'd know where she stood. But
      mostly the child
wants to be The Child.
A child is cared for, a child doesn't go missing,
doesn't get lost in the world, knows who she is,
her mother and father give and guarantee and chip in
      money, put food on the table,
there's somebody to say: child, you will always be My
      Child!
Children don't die; they're safe, young, and cared for.

The parental gods, earthly and otherwise,
shield the children from responsibility and mortality,
smooth the non-negotiability of life and non-life,
saying yada yada yada amen, coo coo coo amen,
stand guard before the past, give the child a sense of
      continuity,
tie us to our ancestors, know the access code,
or so children believe.

No need for protection from the white North or the
      yellow South,

but from the red East, whence demons come crawling
    after dark,
whence blood flows, and from the pitch-black West,
    where death lives,
the child seeks shelter. Here you go,
her mother and father say, a child who heeds her parents
will not be sacrificed to Tlaloc, who devours the bodies of
    children, drinks their blood.

And if she is, you know very well why. Amen.

The child offers the gods her life, her allowance, her
    chocolate, movies,
the world, North, South, West, East.
May she sleep quietly
by the nightlight, since she's afraid of the dark.

Her Mother Calls

Narratrix

Her mother calls her, as she does every day, since her
	daughter doesn't,
and thus she must tighten her blood-bonds, which have
	grown slack.
She pretends to listen, because her mother needs to blather,
and the blathering demands an audience, and her mother
	has only her four walls.
Then the daughter has an idea. She puts down the phone
	and picks up the receiver
every ten minutes and throws in a random *uh-huh* or *yeah*.
She's a little nervous, but it Always Works. Finally, she
	notices
that it's all about the Ear, not about what works or what
	she says,
how to talk trash or shit.
It's all about the Ear. Or the Ear's phantom. The more
	there's *nobody* here,
the better. The simpler, the more let's get this party started,
the nicer the blathering. The chips fly effortlessly into the
	abyss.

The Hellish Infection

Aura as Persephone

I went to see my mother yesterday,
I'm making her cocoa, I ask: One scoop or two?
—It's not enough I sit alone in this room all day,
nobody but the four walls to talk to, but what do you
        know, what do you know of my life,
I live like an animal, like a shadow, I live alone like a
        shadow on the wall of a collapsed building,
but what do you know how much it hurts, where it hurts,
        did you even know I'm in pain,
and it could be my pancreas,
it could be the start of some hellish infection, they'll have
        to do tests.
But what will these tests show? Only death, and still
        they're hard to get through.
Are you getting any of this? You think life's easy,
what difference does it make to you—

And what am I thinking? I'm not thinking anything!
My hands are shaking, I'm shaking all over
and say:

What the fuck, dude? what the fuck?

The Plantation vs. Freedom

Narratrix

Miss Plantation, vs. freedom, she
Has the cultivation of SUFFERING and MOTHERING,
Which they say is inherently good. So,
Sporting her bud of innocence,
Like Rome's heavy-armored legions, the Armada of the
        Catholic Kings,
Like the feathered snake of the Luftwaffe,
She presses on, dives and soars. Tongues scuttling across
        the floors.
And who's this fucking with her now? Who's salting the
        wound? Must be a desperada.
Or some crazy deserter.
Anyway, the slaves, all of them called Dear Child,
Lived in poverty and were lynched for whatever. For
        daring not to call
Five times a week, so not to have to listen to the maw,
And now what's it supposed to do with its gaping?
Alone in its four walls.

Chorus

But however they labor, freedom—either you've got it, or
        you don't.
And that unhappy woman, alone with her four walls!
No satisfaction, no relief, no abolition; the demands keep
        coming.

Neither living, nor dying.

Narratrix
Unrest has come to the slaves' shacks. They whisper and
  conspire.
Whipped up by hormones, they rebel, they want to make
  plans of their own!
Some Nat Turner baits them, incites them. Slaves are
  orphans, he says,
abandoned by gods and men, so what's it to you? You're
  nothing
but a good cut of meat, the flesh that you are, so what's it
  to you?

At night they burst from their shacks with torches, with
  knives and ropes,
they slash burn kill rape, they scream that they're people
  too!
THEY'RE PEOPLE TOO, end slavery now!

"And what's been so bad about Slavery?" Miss Plantation
  wonders. "Didn't I feed you?
Clothe you? Give you Pedialax? Call you 'Uncle Nat'"?
As if you, forgive the comparison, were white, you damn
dirty ape, you faggot, Jew, piece of shit, liberal, traitor,
  punk-ass bitch, Bolshevik pig!

55

Aria
In Self-Help Books They Speak to Us of Reconciliation

Narratrix
In the final burst of desire to be heard. Aura comes
    running
to this deaf larva, to this bloodsucker (sucked dry of
    blood).
To give her a shot at being her mother.
She wants to give her a shot, so that she can forgive her.
And besides, she wants to demand her Admission to
    History.
Her Letting Off the Leash. Her Airing of Grief and
    Grievances
that have always been dismissed with a disbelieving
shriek. One must bid farewell, Aura says,
to the burden of guilt. Enough already with the calling
    every day
and all this four walls bullshit! She would not play the
    fifth.
She also announces that her name is not Adolf Hitler.
Here's ID; you can see the name's different. Has been for
    years.
She demands to be treated with respect!

Hah, now that's what I call the quintessential life crisis.
"Fix this!" it says (unbelievable how long you can hold on
to expectations, and this despite all your experience!). She

doesn't have
too many of them in mind, we have to admit.
She says she's waiting for some kind of *sorry,* so long as it's
        sincere, so long as it knows
what it's really for.
"Aura!" Meter answers. *"YOU SURE KNOW HOW TO
        KICK YOUR MOTHER WHEN SHE'S DOWN,*
And since you're so aggrieved, and since I don't answer
        you as Your Mother,
Kill me now. Just do it!"

*

Kill you, Aura thinks, since the Germans didn't,
two armies at least, Panzer divisions, tanks and air power,
over four years—if they couldn't, how can I?

Bożena Keff

Were Your Tale
(Meter sings bass)

Were your life as tragic as mine
I might be able to talk with you as with someone
Who has a right to exist,
But you don't know these sufferings, and free of these wounds,
       of the essence of life,
Take it, listen, my little bitch.

Now That Hitler

Meter

Now that Hitler, who murdered my family,
And Stalin, may they both rot in Hell, are dead,
You're all I have left, my child,
Of those I have loved.

Aura's Song
By the Rivers of Babylon (2)

(Aura, middle age)
By the rivers of the Babylonian wasteland there I sat down
not remembering and not striking up the band
by the rivers of the wasteland there I sat down listening
as it was all lain waste. The waste's suffering, which cannot
> *be denied, which she blathers on about,*
gives her dominion over all land in her reach,
which she turns into a hell of wasting away
> *into alienation into slavery*
> *into blood(-sucked) ties.*
By the rivers of the Babylonian wasteland there I sat down
"alone with my four walls, tormented by my hellish
> infection,"
without so much as someone to touch.

Being Persephone

Narratrix
Aura's hair is now gray, but unlike her mother, she dyes.
Aura visits her after a long absence to see how her mother's
getting on in life, in this, the new age's old age.
They've sipped their tea, sit quietly, watch TV
about their country. They're erecting a monument to
      Dmowski. Mother says: look,
everywhere, bastard Fascism, always these bastards.
When I was young, they ran through Lvov with razors
      and slashed Jews,
now the Jews are all gone, all killed, the rest driven out. I
      regret having stayed
(though what do you do people are stupid helpless idiotic).
But for these nationalists nothing's changed. They appoint
      their own Jews.
Their morality is something that allows them to slash
      others with razors,
that's all they get out of it, and again they're rinsing their
      mouths
from morning to night with fatherland and god. They
      don't deserve a single Jew here,
whatever his nation, gender, orientation, or skin color.
I have no idea how decent people get on
in this country, perhaps when Europe opens up they'll leave,
or they must suffer. I, for my part, as you know, believe in
      no god.

I'm a realist; self-delusion is, in my circumstances, beneath
    me.
Believe me. Maybe I talk about it too much, but I've lived
    through too much, too.

To which Aura says: Being Persephone, I agree with you,
    Hecate,
And I must declare you to be a person of honor.

PART VII
THESE MOTHERS
ARE PATRIARCHAL

The Mother's Lot

Persephone
My comrade in feminist arms, a woman with the jaws of
    a wolf
(she's sentimental toward matriarchal religion, that she
    herself may become Goddess,
the ur-mother of women everywhere), says: Such is the
    mother's lot.
These are patriarchal mothers, by which I mean to say
That patriarchy has made them empty and cold, packed
    with ice,
And, like ice, fragile. It's not their fault alone.
Fault rests in their having been raised without respect,
That they have no respect for their gender,
And therefore for that of their daughters.

This truth is real. But incomplete, and thus skewed,
and I cannot stand it! The Mother is a human being,
so that I wish to say that a person is more than her gender,
age, or color, someone more, and cannot consent to any
    reduction
that would render mothers innocent as victims of Father
    Patriarchus.
The patriarchal mother reveals the Myth of the Mother,
    and when she avails herself of it
it gives her a sense of ownership over the product

attained through (a certain) control of the means of
      reproduction,
she imposes herself on it, she smothers it, chokes it on
      guilt and obligation,
she pays for it with a hope so dim you can neither live
      with it nor die from it,
it allows for the permanent production of the child in the
      child, that it might produce the mother in her,
that the Mother not lose her property and power. The
      child is a secret workforce
from the lands of the mentally and emotionally retarded:
it is always reproducing the range of her power.

Aristotle says: The slave is born of slave parents.
And this principle rings true to this day.

Persephone
To which we must answer: Surely, O comrade in women's
      affairs, surely.
Patriarchy has packed her with ice, yet sometimes it is
      they who wish to frost over.
This does not all happen without their consent!

Narratrix
Surely, what could her mother's mother, Sabina, do with
    this late child?
She'd given everything to Nola's brother, her firstborn.
All her feelings, all her money, to save him from the cabbala
he'd fallen into for the ideal of equality, justice,
and non-discrimination called communism, and while he
    sat in his cell
with his twenty comrades she'd bring rolls and coffee for
    them all,
the only way he would eat. She had nothing left for her,
he'd already taken it all, and then came ruin. Nola lived
in exile with her stingy, rich aunt and in time became
the charge and nanny for her own brother, seventeen years
    her senior,
too much to be her brother, too little to be her father,
she had to go through adult life in diapers too seldom
    changed.

Persephone
And what comes next? The same thing, always the same, if
    allowed.
But the war came, and everyone was killed.
(Because of her eternal babbling,
to this day I don't know what this means to me.)

So there's patriarchy in the picture, that much is clear.
There's even an ultra-patriarchal war. But what happens to
    man?
Where to find a modicum of insight,
respect for the child, even a bit of sympathy? I won't even
    mention empathy.
Don't you know, Ms. Wolf-Jaw?

Surely.
There is evil in patriarchy. But there are also its margins,
the matriarchal spheres. Patriarchy is the most general
    definition of slavery.
It is its principal patrix, and at its edges: the matrix.

And the Fathers?

Narratrix and Aura: A Duet

We also wish to say that it's not because there shouldn't be
    any Fathers
In the picture that there *are* none. There should be, no
    question.
There should be, most of all because their absence
    absolves them.
And how easy it is to forgive them once they've forgiven
    themselves!
The son chewed up and spat out, the daughter spat out
    from the get-go, and still they're free,
For they feel themselves drawn to other worlds.
To the ideal, unfettered from the world, to hammering
    against the void,
To their own frustration, to envy, to the rituals of power
    and priesthood,
To rendering the corpus incorporeal, to winning or, if not,
    losing.
To pouring it down the gullet or sticking it in the vein,
    whatever your poison.
And they abandoned their children to the Mother, since
    there's no one like her.
They threw the child into Tlaloc's maw, a cunning move!

Fathers, mothers—what do these names even mean? What
    words are these?

We call for these names to be abolished! All hail the era
Of proper names!

Aura
Please let it be understood
That our father falls beyond the frame of the present story.
But that's just us.

Part VIII
L'Humanité

Draft of a Manifesto
(John Lennon, "Imagine")

Narratrix
So what if humankind were suddenly to get it, that it's
          alone,
that there's nothing beyond it but sky above and earth
          below?
And feel responsible for itself? And empathetic enough
at least not to murder itself or multiply like crazy?
And give itself, its own history, other species, the Earth, a
          chance?
Be mutually more inclusive than exclusive?
Expand on the four colors of skin and two sexes, elevate
          the alien,
bring youth and age together, because they couldn't get
          further apart,
sufficiency instead of wealth and poverty; everywhere we
          need change
and responsibility,
that's how I see it.

                    *

And while we're at it, maybe the human species should see
          itself through its ally's eyes.
Keep confidence with the dog, the monkey, the turtle?
And call itself *L'Humanité*, like the newspaper?

Persephone

And what am I supposed to do, here like everybody else
      by accident,
not really from here, this is just my address, but it's always
shelter in illness and out of the rain.

I assumed my path from my parents.
But I don't know if they'd know it.
I'm destined to be at once alien
and near at hand.

Epilogue

Song of the Waiting Room

(note the words from a popular songbook)

Narratrix
I'm sitting in the waiting room to see
The physical therapist, because banging out
These shameful poems on my computer has messed up
    my upper back,
And the old folks next to me are carrying on
A deafening conversation.

Lady 1
I adore this one singer, you know, the one who sings
    funny old bits,
he's really skinny, curly hair, what's his name?
Lovely voice! What's it … Grossek?

Gentleman 1
Oh yeah, curly hair, flaxen locks, ha ha. Have to admit,
He has quite a voice—and when one of *them* has a voice,
    he knows how to sell it.
My sister's boy's voice is nicer, but you won't see him on TV!

Lady 2
Do you even get to see a Pole anymore
On Polish television? Do we have Polish newspapers in
    Poland?

More like Yiddish-zeitung.

Gentleman 2
Like those kosher papers are so democratic, like they're so
    disgusted
With dictatorship. And who financed Stalin
If not those Jewish bankers? And Hitler, too, until…

Gentleman 1
You're wrong there! They never stopped, they kept paying
Till the very end. Anyway, it's common knowledge
Hitler's grandmother was Jewish. I got it straight from the
    Talmud.
Which is very anti-Poland, by the way. I have a
    subscription to the Talmud.

Chorus of Patients
It's common knowledge that Hitler's grandmother was a Jew!

Jews—Kikes! And the Germans are Jews! And the
    Russkies are yids!

Lady 2
Historians are coming to a consensus that in the Warsaw
    Ghetto
There was neither hunger, nor disease.

They had it pretty good in there, and then
They broadcast to the world that they'd been murdered.

Lady 1
That's because they're all *pro-life*, get it?
But only *pro-* their own. Nowadays they're the ones
        peddling
Birth-control pills and condoms....

Gentleman 2
My dear lady! They only peddle them to others.
But they multiply. They say we have anti-Semitism
        without Jews in Poland,
But how can they have it any other way, when they hide
        like moles?

Lady 2
If there weren't so many of them, if they weren't in
        control,
This country would look different. You think our
        pensions
Would be so laughable? Would there be unemployment?

Gentleman 1
The pig is holding the bag and squealing. Squealing about
        how during the war

Poles allegedly burned them in barns,
Persecuted them, gave them into German hands.

Lady 2
I heard from my
Uncle how during the war this one old Jew killed an entire
    Polish family,
A dozen or more people, to avenge their taking
His silver candlesticks. Which they'd only done
To hold onto them for those yids.
It happened right under the Germans' noses! Why don't
    the papers write about that?

Chorus of Patients
Because they're not Polish. Jews are the only ones who
    sling mud at Poles,
while others shower them with medals and honors. Like
    Miłosz, i.e., a poet
with such admiration for kikes and pederasts, and that
    Szymborska.

*

Jewish fags! And Jewish dykes, and those hook-nosed
    feminazis!

Gentleman 1
And now they just go on and on

about asking the Jews' forgiveness, which everyone knows
    their president, Stolzman, has done already.
Forgiveness how, and what for? Maybe ask their
    forgiveness
For murdering all those Palestinians, worse than anything
The Nazis or the Gestapo ever did to them!

Lady 2
They're worse than the Gestapo or the NKVD, which
    they invented, anyway,
It's their job, and no one else's, to ask forgiveness for their
    treachery,
For the blood in the matzo, for their Jew-communism,
    their secret police, their capitalism,
For their pederasts, who parade around
Our city, which white people built,
With their asses hanging out like baboons!

Gentleman 2
And let them finally ask forgiveness for martyring Jesus! I
    go to church.
And I saw the movie! Let their president come to our
    president
On his knees. Let him come crawling all the way to
    Częstochowa.
Let them thank us for letting their ashes rest on our land,

Which we provide them without payment or interest!
But let them pay us our due, at last,
Because a thank-you's not going to cut it.

Lady 2
Please, let them ask forgiveness and pay us back! But let
        them say thank you, too!
For a millennium of hospitality,
During which they grew fat off our land, drank from our
        waters,
And robbing us blind! While we protected them and, with
        an open hand, gave them rights,
Our country has been like a mother to them!

Choir
The country was like a Mother to them, like their own
        Mother.
And a mother deserves her due!

*

The Braves are a bunch of kikes!
The Indians are a bunch of yids!
The Redskins are a bunch of Jews!

Proper Names

The work that is *On Mother and Fatherland* is to navigate the historical and the mythic in their connection to personal experience and collective memory. The names of mythic and historical figures therefore haunt the text and are invoked to cross purposes by its antagonists. In similar manner, throughout the postwar period heroes of Jewish resistance to Nazism—people like **Mordechai Anielewicz**, who led and perished in the Warsaw Ghetto Uprising—were simultaneously glorified by survivors, Jewish and Polish alike, and vilified by nationalists. In fact, the latter resumed the prewar practice of disparaging their adversaries, whether a rival political party or a rival sports team, by calling them Jews. It is a practice that remains common in Poland today. Thus **KOR** (*Komitet Obrony Robotników,* or the Workers' Defense Committee), a forerunner to the anti-Communist Solidarity movement, was targeted as an anti-Polish, Zionist conspiracy. Journalists who look critically at Poland's past and present, whether in league with the Communist leadership in the 1980s (**Mieczysław Rakowski, Jerzy Urban**) or opposed to the same (**Adam Michnik, Seweryn Blumsztajn, Jacek Kuroń**), are inevitably dismissed by some for their Jewish roots, however distant or even fictive. As in the West, the fantasy of a Jewish conspiracy, especially in the media, has proven difficult to dispel. To nationalists, Poland's highest-circulation newspaper, *Gazeta Wyborcza,* is *Gazeta Koszerna*—"**the kosher paper**"; its president, Aleksander Kwaśniewski (in office 1995–2005), is really a Jew named **Izaak Stoltzman**. Such nonsense is an ever-present, if marginal, feature of social and political reality.

83

About the Author

BOŻENA KEFF was born in 1948 in Warsaw, where she currently resides. A lecturer in Gender Studies at the University of Warsaw, she is also a research associate of the Jewish Historical Institute. In addition to three previous books of poetry, she is the author, most recently, of *Anti-Semitism: An Unfinished History* (2013) and (as Bożena Umińska) *Figure with Shadow: Portraits of Jewish Women in Polish Literature* (2001). She contributes regularly to Poland's leading magazines.

About the Translators

ALISSA VALLES is the author of the poetry books *Orphan Fire* (2008) and *Anastylosis,* a book-length poem published in a thermal paper edition for an exhibition at the Whitechapel Art Gallery in London in 2014; she edited and co-translated Zbigniew Herbert's *Collected Poems* (2007) and *Collected Prose* (2010). Her translarion of Ryszard Krynicki's *Our Life Grows* will appear at NYRB Poets in 2017.

BENJAMIN PALOFF is the author of the poetry collections *And His Orchestra* and *The Politics,* and of a critical volume, *Lost in the Shadow of the Word* (Space, Time, and Freedom in Interwar Eastern Europe). His translations include, most recently, Richard Weiner's *The Game for Real.* He teaches at the University of Michigan.